Mexican Mosaics

Lester Hirsh

Mexican Mosaics

Lester Hirsh

Parisburg Publishing
Pennsylvania, USA

ISBN: 978-1-61918-023-9

Parisburg Publishing
Pennsylvania, USA
www.parisburg.com

Dedication

To members of the Hirsh and Vanier family and friends

Contents

Artists   67

Author   71

Preface

My first trip to Mexico City commenced January 20th, 1999. I was invited to a family Bar Mitzvah, the son of my cousin Enrique Vanier Hirsh. I spent all of four days there minus six hours. It was enough to wet the palette but not to sustain it. My ear was beginning to sense nuance in the Spanish language. The rhythms danced in my head like the canvas of colors in the surroundings. The architecture of buildings, cobblestone streets, the market place, restaurants, clothes, expressions on forlorn and happy faces. One young Mexican señorita reminded me of Michelle Pfeiffer.

I observed and listened intently. I reveled in the sense of close knit families. It is the custom in Latin and European culture that families live together and stay close throughout their lives. I was a foreigner in this land but felt familiar in some sense of longing. Yet not all the romance of discovery could exclude other realities. For instance, I was told people avoid police. Especially, if you are driving. They have been known to be like denizens in the dark, often as criminal as the criminal elements they are hired to protect good citizens from.

Yet, the irony is this fear lives alongside the atmosphere of fiesta and abounding beauty. This beauty basks in the cafes and parks, in the landscape of greenery, mountains, and sight of the desert cactus. In the volcanoes, and landscaped homes with palatial gardens. In the museums, archeological sights and even the dusty corridors of the barrio district. In the cathedrals and temples, and sidewalk carnivals. In the marketplace where art of all kinds is displayed and feasted on by international tourists.

It all pulled me in like a horse to a watering well. I could hardly imagine a day gone by without jotting a poem, setting a lyric to music, or sketching a crooked design on some canvas. I sensed that as the poet Lorca suggested, by knowing another culture I would better understand myself. I want to know more of Mexico, again and again. Bueno. Hasta luego.

1/27/99

Lester Hirsh

The poem
The song
The picture
Is only water
Drawn from the well
Of the people
And it should be given back
To them in a cup of beauty
So that they may drink
And in drinking,
Understand themselves.

— Federico Garcia Lorca
20th century poet/playwright

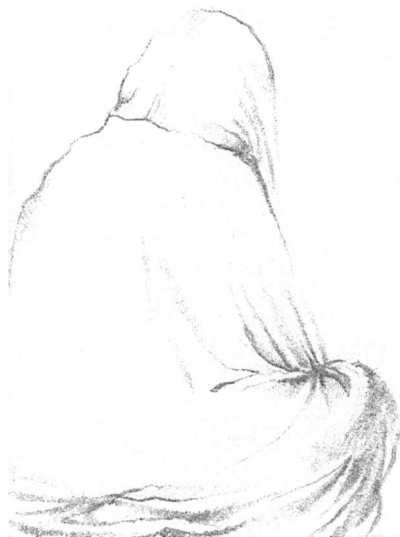

Untitled / Joseph McCann

Acknowledgments:

Special thanks to Nelly Zamora Jones for her diligent effort beyond the call of duty to translate 15 pages of poems and impressions into her native Spanish language. I thank Nelly for her superb creations of art-sophisticated, surreal, spiritual, and superbly crafted at the same time. Nelly, you are a treasured friend and inspiring artist. You motivate me to extend my creative efforts beyond the realm of any ordinary complacency.

Special thanks to my beloved and endearing friend Raquel Fruchter, an artist who has overcome the extraordinary adversities in life, created wonderful warm paintings full of pathos for the plight of the poor, as well as an appreciation for the beauty of landscapes, the large canvas of life. Thanks Raquel, for lending me your fine work for the Mexican Mosaics and for creating a home away from home for this troubadour poet when he visits Tampa in the winter months.

Thanks again to Joe McCann, exquisite artist and friend, for his classic drawing, sense of humor, fine homespun spaghetti meals and hospitality. My humble appreciation for the tours of Tampa- from the art museums to the Lowery Zoo, the Library and Cuban restaurant, the University of South Florida campus, Barnes & Noble bookstore and Gulf of Mexico Saint Petersburg white sand beaches.

Thanks again to Walter Dolen, publisher of Parisburg publishing, for his timely attention to meeting the timeline for the first printing of the Mexican Mosaics, and the acquired skills to accomplish the task.

Solitude / **Nelly Zamora Jones**

Looking Back at Mexico City

I sit in my abode in a demure town by the train tracks in Pennsylvania. Mexico City is fifteen years in the rear view mirror. I was 48 then, a year after recovering from open heart surgery. My mother was 85 and had survived a few surgeries of her own. Still, it would have been ill-advised for her to travel to Mexico at her age. I elected to go. So too, did my brother, sister, and sister-in-law.

Looking back on that journey, the memory of those moments are less lucid than they were then. The film has faded to sepia. There is more nuance than specifics to recall. That is why I am glad to have written the initial impressions and poems in the immediate moment, to capture the essence of it all. Granted they were not monumental pieces, but collectively create a picture clear as a photo taken and recorded. Adding art work from my friends Raquel Fruchter and Nelly Zamora Jones, and journal notes before the trip, fill in the open spaces. It is my hope that any reader, family, or friend, can appreciate the spirit and intention of these creations. If possible, think of these pieces as journalistic notes- a sketchbook to digest at any given time.

The poems cover a range of events: Hacienda de los Morales — a Mexico City restaurant; a trip to a museum; the city hall; an evening with Beatriz Ezban, the artist; eating Alegria- a Mexican candy bar; Ramat Shalom, the synagogue; Un Nuevo Concepto En Café- A Coffee Station; Impressions on the architecture of buildings and mountains in the background; panhandling and prostitutes on the streets; reflections on the Pope's pending visit at the time. Between taking notes I was busy with events as they were planned for the Bar Mitzvah of my cousin Enrique's son. I either wrote early in the morning or late at night after everyone retired. I wrote with a penchant for recording the moment, and attention to detail.

I didn't write about Nachama Vanier's home- the matriarch of the family who settled there from Lithuania escaping World War II. I remember her home in the downtown district. It was warm, full of family pictures, furnishings and Jewish themes like the menorah on the table. I was named after her uncle Lester, my grandfather, who sent letters, savings, and clothing to his Mexican relative in the difficult days of the War years. Nachama also adored my father, Max Hirsh. She would gaze at me and see the mirror of his image in my eyes. I didn't write about this, or my stay at Enrique and Betty's home on the hill on the outskirts of the city. Nor did I write about the Sunday morning visit to the outdoor market.

I remember being at the market with my sister Barbara, my relatives, Marta, Betty, Betsheva and her daughter Sandra. Marta bought me an Aztec belt I still own but can't get around my burgeoning waist line. I bought a miniature wooden violin and bow which is perched on the wall of my bedroom.

I believe we toured the Frida Kahlo house museum. How could I forget that or confuse it with the movie starring Salma Hayek, as the artist Frieda, and Alfred Molina, as Diego Rivera. That is the warp of time playing tricks on the mind. One thing I can't forget is the night Montezuma's Revenge hit me when I returned to New Hampshire. I had to leave a beginning computer class because of the nausea and subsequent sickness that grounded me for 24 hours.   Lester Hirsh-6/1/2014

The Mexico City Journal

The trip began before the arrival as all journeys begin. In this case, back a few months when I first put to task the notion this trip was predestined. Perhaps it began in the subconscious mind when I lived in Miami in the 1960's and 1970's. Dade County had an influx of Latin culture. There, my brother Joe met, and would later marry Katia Miranda. I was paying more attention to the cultural divide. Turning back to my childhood recollections in Pennsylvania, there was the auspicious book, B'Chor Ben B'Chor (Eldest Son of an Eldest Son) written by uncle Ben Hirsh. The chronology, and legacy of the Hirsh family - our roots, not unlike Alex Haley's Roots.   In 1950 Uncle Ben wrote and published 500 to 1,000 copies of the family book that spanned over three generations, back to the great grandparents roots in Lithuania. It was in that book and in subsequent conversations with my father that I learned of my Mexican relatives- Nachama, who emigrated to Mexico from Lithuania. Nachama, born in 1914, at the family homestead in Pamoosha, was the only member of her immediate family to escape World War II, and the Hitler invasion. Since that time the next generation of in laws has spawned like Salmon in the stream.

A few months ago I saw my cousin Enrique Vanier in Miami. It was Thanksgiving week. We all dined together. Enrique's son Ricardo's Bar Mitzvah would be held January 21, 1999. My invitation would be sent out. I responded, "yes, I'd like to go." As Goethe noted when we put forth that notion providence takes over. I departed Concord New Hampshire before the sun rise. At 5 in the morning, Brian Pfitzer drove down with me to the Logan Airport in Boston in my Sentra. I arrived there before 6:30 a.m, well in time for my 8:45 a.m. departure. Having had but a few hours' sleep, the night before and having gone through a medical procedure and 24 hour fast, I was a bit exhausted and weary.

The plane left on time and after breakfast I slept some in between reading Mailer's book on Picasso. We arrived in Miami around 12:20 pm and shortly thereafter I made my way to gate E-24 where the Mexico City Flight would depart. I called my 85 year old mother on my calling card and spoke a few minutes. Leaning into the pay phone I disconnected it and had to call her back. After taking care of this courtesy call and receiving last minute notes from mother about what to do and not do, I readied for boarding. The plane was an 8 seater- a Boeing with the teleprompter machines and more space in which to walkabout. The first flight was a smaller plane though the flight was good.

I found myself seated next to a young woman from Caracas Venezuela. At first I thought she was from Minnesota. I understood her but with all the Spanish being spoken around me since arriving in Miami it was no surprise. This was a moment of comic relief. I said to her- "Minnesota- home of Garrison Keillor." She responded with that perplexed look- "I've never been to Minnesota. I'm from Venezuela." "Oh, I returned. I have a friend whose sister lives in Caracas. I hear it's a nice place." By now everything seemed awkward. I began to write in my Mexican journal. After some 10 minutes before departure, the young woman realized the flight was not full so she excused herself to take a seat in the center aisle. She proceeded to lay her head back on a pillow, her legs folded one over the other and like an angel she slept. Anticipating the magnitude of the trip I was embarking upon I just felt that empty space like the silent sounds of meditation. The flight had begun and Mexico City would lie three hours and forty five minutes flight time ahead. 1/20/99

Impressions of Mexico City Prior to My Arrival

1. A burgeoning city so packed with people that the aesthetic amenities are outweighed by the crisis of density.

2. The city by a Volcano 7,500 feet above sea level. The air quality will be dangerous, the pollution unbearable.

3. A sense of hustle like any teeming metropolis. It's hard to imagine tranquil enclaves scattered amidst the concrete jungle.

4. Dirty streets but much nightlife. Tortillas and pop sold by street vendors. Hustlers of all kinds waiting to rip off strangers.

5. Beautiful senoritas everywhere.

6. Poverty and squalors on the cities edge.

7. A large modern airport. A potentially dangerous place like the criminal taxis service.

8. Some dauntingly beautiful places- Aztec and Mayan architecture.

9. A very discrete but nice Jewish community and temples.

10. Evidence of a Catholic country everywhere. Crucifix on mountain tops, in store fronts, on street walkers.

1/20/99
lh

Thirty minutes out of Mexico City tourist visas are passed out. Unfortunately, the airline ran out of visas written in English, so I received one in Spanish and had a hard time making out all the details. How I wish I spoke fluent Spanish. I can see the Mexican mountains out the window of the plane. They remind me of the Rockies. They edge up into the clouds. They are fairly barren. I am tired of breathing stale air in the plane. My venture is approaching. With the plane bouncing around I feel I'm getting motion sickness. I should have taken those motion sickness pills. I haven't been in a plane this long in a while. I feel my thoughts are as thin as the air. This is not good.

Two days later I feel some of my ignorance of Mexico City has been dispelled. I realize how close knit the Jewish Community is here and the significant family I have south of the border. In two days I have seen some of the city, visited a museum, shopping centers, the orthodox Synagogue, seen panhandlers on the streets, eaten in simple and refined elegance, a variety of Mexican cuisine, and most importantly gotten to know some of my relatives and their friends, and even fine- tuned my ear to Spanish. I've met an artist and perhaps made a friend and contemplate a return visit here.

1/20/99 and 1/22/99
lh

John's Pass / Raquel Fruchter

Mexico City Mosaics

Café on a Mexican corner
Chatter like crickets
Teeming sounds of city
All the world is one

Chikita bonita
Mexican pop music
Mexico City in motion

Mexican hills
Mayan Gods in the sky
Watch over people
Like morning sun
Coming out
Of night shadows

1/22/97

Alegria

Alegria means joy
it is made of Amaranto seed
this sweet bar
the size of an eraser
a solid block
of compact seed
has one raisin
and a walnut
set in the center
to add flavor
like a worm
in Tequilla

Sold as a candy bar
by street vendors
Alegria is a pleasant
and popular sidewalk snack
in Mexico City

1/22/99

Room With A View

browns and greens
sepia on the
concrete skyscrapers
modest for the modern age

ivory discs- TV antenna
orange colored condos
cars of all colors

staring down the avenue
de los Bosques
basking in the view

a painters palette
by any stretch
of imagination

1/23/99

Street Parking / Raquel Fruchter

Hacienda de los Morales

This posh Mexican restaurant
looks like a museum
a dignified bit of antiquity
with a courtyard
impressionistic paintings
in fine wooden or metal frames.

There are tables in the round
for large family dining
patrons are serenaded
by strolling Mariachi musicians.

Among the delicacies
are fried worms, often eaten
in rolled soft shells
with enchilatta
or a pate mushroom filing.

The rich dine here
in the house of Morales
Morales being a surname
of one of the patrons
of the wealthy class.

The menu is diverse
pasta, fish, meat,
served with vegetables,
salad and soup.
There are a variety
of desserts,
cake, pie, and tarts.

Located near Mexico City's
exclusive shopping district,
it is one of many
contrasting views
of a city alive with
mention of the muse,
of beauty and sadness,
poverty and wealth, cohabiting like a gar fish
on a mamouth host

1/24/99

The Power of Metaphor

In the National Palace, a fresco,
alive on the wall, like a lizard crawling,
the Aztec world of Diego Rivera, is fixed
a finite measure, deceptive
as Merlin with a magical scent
beyond a tangible document

Portentious roles, the Mexican Revolution
from a Spanish invasion
to the workers liberation
on an adjacent wall, the Marxist call
the triptych is emblazoned
like the colors of fall

Sentinels stand erect
beneath the ceiling
by a courtyard entrance
in the corridors of the palace

Tourists are drawn day long
by Rivera's artful hand
or the sense of contraband
a notion, politically potent

Guards in green fatigues
with automatic rifles strapped
are kept in line and casual step
preserving law and order

yet, the mural feeds
a curious fever
to the skeptic and believer
while the militia makes
an odd buttress plank
dining on
ideology and art
like a viper and flute
under the same roof

1/31/99

Allegory of a Painting, "Swan Song" / Nelly Zamora Jones

Miller on Mexican Minds

Henry Miller, in the minds
of Mexican artists,
a hero I am told,
Tropic of Cancer,
Capricorn, and more
bore their imprint
like Leonard Cohen's music
hot sauce, tortillas,
taste of passion
on the tongue
tequila with a worm
down the perennial pipe

1/24/99

Plumes of Smoke

Active volcano in view
steam rising like
ancient ruins
in a morning sky

Airport runway waits
for plumes of smoke
to enter her

The past breathes
like a bad dream
revenge of the inquisition
conquistadores

1/24/99

La Buena Tierra

The good earth has seedlings
trees standing proud,
mountains bald and breathing,
reaching more than a mile high
toward the sky.

On top of this lake
more than 20 million skate
in cars, on foot,
whatever it takes
for the earth to hold
and not condemn
on top of this lake
20 million lives transcend.

The good earth growls
like a hungry child
a mindful mouth
that needs to be fed.

The good earth hides
no lie for long.
Two active volcanoes
stare down her valley.

The good earth hides
no lie for long,
like an eye down a gun barrel,
20 million martyrs
sing her song.

The good earth rumbles
like thunder and lightning
from earthquakes beneath
her watering pools.

La Buena Tierra
is mindful of duty
but has not the scrutiny
of people it keeps.

The good earth goes on
like a melody sung
a tune we all know
to the valley below.
1/24/99

Pueblo / **Raquel Fruchter**

Then the Pope Spoke

Inside a served bag of Ruffles Potato Chips
this square sticker sat for all eyes to view:

Joven:
No Permitas
Que La Violencia
Destruya
La Vida Y
La Libertad
Del Ser Humano

Juan Pablo II

This message on a small square paper
in the snack bag for lunch
dispersed to passengers
on our American Flight
from Mexico City to Dallas
came as the Pope
was soon to lead Sunday Mass
in Mexico City
January 24, 1999

The weekend of the 22nd of January
marked the Pope's fourth visit this year
to this Catholic country
which gives more financial support
to the Vatican than any country
on our planet

It was rumored to be
the safest weekend
to walk the city streets

The day and night before Mass
I saw prostitutes in red skirts
on the corners of their downtown district
I saw street peddlars- children
selling Trident gum-
a woman juggling

in the stress of traffic-
children washing car windows
panhandling change-
People were encamped
in central square
across from the Presidential Palace-
but I saw no acts of violence
the weekend the Pope came to town
and though I saw not the holy man
his words appeared in a bag of potato chips
as I flew from Mexico to Dallas Texas
you might say, his words,
were food for thought...
1/24/99

Homeless / **Raquel Fruchter**

Beatriz Ezban

A petite modern painter
once studied in Monet,
the classics, and more
has also been inspired
by William Blake,
Henry Miller,
Herman Melville,
the songs of Leonard Cohen,
to name but a few.

Her work has been juried
throughout Mexico,
Iceland, Westchester Pennsylvania,
Hong Kong, and elsewhere.

She is of Syrian Jewish descent,
a native of Mexico,
her studio home,
in downtown Mexico City.

Having met through cousins,
Beatriz and Enrique,
we strolled the streets
a few hours,
sat in sidewalk cafes,
and found the common
touch points of people,
the universal pains
and joys of life.

"The language is different
   but peoples wants and needs
   the same everywhere,"
   she revealed.

Later, sipping herbal tea
in the delicate hours
we talked of Malcolm Lowry's
Under the Volcano-

Gabriel Garcia Marquez,
Octavio Paz,
Elizabeth Bishop,
Leon Felipe,
Isabel Allende,
Henry Miller,
more poets, painters, weavers of tales,
as a Leonard Cohen tape
played Everybody Knows behind us
and the night like all nights
slipped quietly away.

1/26/99

Beatriz Ezban: Born in Mexico City and awarded the acquisition prize of the XI Painting Biennale Rufino Tamayo in August 2002, with her painting Babel, Beatriz has an extensive career as an artist.

Between 1975 and 2003, she has participated in more than 80 national and international group exhibits. Since 1986, she has presented more than thirty individual exhibits throughout Mexico, Iceland, Ireland, Norway, Canada, Spain, United States, Poland, Romania, Serbia and Germany, which led to the selection of her work as part of the group of the 33 most outstanding artists of the country that formed part of the Permanent Collection at the Official Residence of the Pinos in Mexico, among other important collections.

Beatriz Ezban is one of the main exponents of abstract painting in Mexico, for which this exhibit is an excellent opportunity to enjoy her work.

Ramat Shalom

This orthodox synagogue
on the avenue Loma del Bosque
is situated on the hilly
western side of the city

In this end of town
an enclave of Jewish residents
reside

There is a downtown district
where many Jewish merchants
set up shop and settled
before, during, and after
World War II

There are about 55,000 Jews
in Mexico, the majority
of which, some 40,000
live in Mexico City

Ramat Shalom is one
of the four to six Temples
in the city
rebuilt in the early 1990's
it is as modern as any
American prototype

Women are separated from men
as orthodox tradition instructs it
is difficult in this day
for many of the female spouses
to accept the prayer that
men recite when they
don the tefillin
on their arm
and doven or pray
thanking God
each day
for not making them
a woman

At Ramat Shalom as in most Latin culture, regardless of religion- orthodoxy is the norm. In the Jewish community it is still predominant in Mexico City as tradition has firm roots. The congregants also have their own militia, so to speak. There are volunteer men by the shul and close street corners- who stand guard on the Sabbath. Vigilance is an imperative.

1/27/99

Un Nuevo Concepto En Cafes (Coffee Station)

Beatriz Ezban and I
drank coffee and chatted
at this Coffee Station

with chairs and benches
and gnarled metal coffee dispensers
extending like vines, an artful design

It was the kind of station stop
a writer would take
and make the most of
with the power of a pen
and observation

Every city has its monuments
its broken down corners
crevices, crannies,
and nooks

the barrios, bistros,
cathedrals,
parks,
and shopping districts

    an artists eye
    finds a nest
    some place to rest
    to invite a moveable feast

    Un Nuevo Concepto En Cafes
    was one perch
    for Señor Hirsh

1/27/99

Wild Ginger / Raquel Fruchter

Snapshot

The tourist saw the turrets,
terra cotta tile rooftops,
cupolas, ornamental artifacts,
on churches, museum fronts,
governments buildings-

The weather-worn limestone
facades by the squares
and corridors of back streets
that looked somewhat sad-

But not near as sad
as the sight of children,
old women, young men
on the streets-
selling gum, candy,
flowers, peanuts,
dolls and ballons,
or an organ grinder
extending for pocket change,
or the woman who juggled
like a clown in the midst
of oncoming traffic
or kids who washed car windows
the decrepit woman on her knees
reaching like Michelangelo's hand
in the Sistine Chapel,
for some heavenly reprieve-

The tourist could not think
of Mexican peasants
as marionettes in a museum
or click the Polaroid with pride

Like palaces and art
they were a breathing part
of history, past and present,
woven into the fabric of urbanity,
of Mexico City, the Third World,
the world beyond these borders

1/3/99

Todos Santos

In the museum
were masks and marionettes
trees of life and death
a band of skeletons
playing drums and clarinet

The festival of death
is treated like a grand exit
not just a commemoration
but a grand reunion too

Souls of dead children
return on the day
before Todos Santos

In the month of November
as Aztec custom goes
the 9th month is dedicated
to souls of infants
the 10th month
to adults

The festival begins
on October 31
the day of angelitos,
or little angels

The pageantry unravels
by the feast of San Andres
or the end of November
leading into December

Todos Santos
is All Saints Day
with painted skeleton suits
and Grim Reaper scythes on display

In this way
the culture honors souls
living and departed
wearing similar clothes

2/13/99

Aztec Woman / Raquel Fruchter

Touchdown

The plane came out of the sky
into this airport
modest in size

for the worlds largest city
nearly 22 million souls
the embodiment of perpetuidad
in the valley below

the active volcano
the uncertain earth
we touched down
as we left
more full and rebirthed

1/21/99

Spanish Traducción

Lester Hirsh / Nelly Zamora Jones

Prefacio

Mi jornada empezó en la Ciudad de Méjico el 20 de Enero de 1999. Yo fui invitado
a la celebración de edad (BarMitzvah) de mi primo Enrique Vanier Hirsh. Yo me quedé cuatro días, menos seis horas con ellos. Fue bastante para saborear el paladar, pero no lo suficiente como para sostener mi apetito. Mis oídos empezaban a distinguir esos sonidos de la lengua castellana. Los ritmos bailaban en mi cabeza como lienzos de pinturas por todos mis alrededores. La arquitectura española tallada de piedras en sus edificios y calles, los mercados, restaurantes, vestuarios y expresiones felices de sus caras. Una señorita mejicana me recordó a la actriz Michelle Pfeiffer.

Yo observé y oí con atención. Me maravillé con el concepto de la unidad familiar. Es una costumbre latina y europea que las familias se queden unidas por el resto de sus vidas. Yo era el extranjero en esta tierra que sentía algo familiar que me atraía y que también lo añoraba. Aunque ningún otro romance descubierto podría excluir mi realidad. Por ejemplo, me habían dicho que las gentes evitan a la policía, especialmente cuando uno maneja. Que ellos tienen la fama de ser como naturalizados en la oscuridad, o como los criminales en la noche con sus elementos de criminales para proteger al buen ciudadano.

Sin embargo, la ironía era el vivir con temor entre una atmosfera de fiesta y abundancia de belleza. Esta belleza se soleaba en los cafés y parques, en los valles verdes, montañas y las vistas de sus cactus en el desierto. También en los volcanes y en sus casas y con sus jardines suntuosos. En los museo, en los descubrimientos arqueológicos y hasta en los pasillos de los barrios en el distrito. En sus catedrales y en sus templos, en sus aceras festivas de carnaval. En los mercados donde sus artesanías de todas clases están para festejar al turista internacional.

Todo alrededor me halaba como un caballo que va a un pozo por agua. Yo casi no podría imaginarme sin escribir una poesía al día, escribir las liricas de una canción, o un diseño con líneas torcidas sobre un lienzo. Yo me sentí como el poeta, Lorca que sugirió, que al conocer otras culturas uno puede llegar a conocerse mejor a si mismo. Yo quiero saber mas de Méjico, otra vez, y otra vez. Bueno. Hasta Luego.

1/27/99
Lester Hirsh

Traducción por Nelly Zamora Jones, 11 de Junio del 2014

La poesía
La canción
La pintura
Es solamente agua
Sacada del pozo
De la población
Debe regresarles a ellos
En una taza hermosa
La bebida que solo
Ellos puedan entender.

Federico García Lorca
Siglo 20, Poeta/Dramaturgo

Mosaicos

Mosaicos en la Ciudad de Méjico

El café en una esquina de Méjico
Conversaciones como grillos
En campeonatos entre ellos
Sonidos de la ciudad se oyen
Todo el mundo es Uno

Chiquita bonita
Música pop Mejicana
Movimiento Mejicano

Las montañas de Méjico
Con sus Dioses Mayas
Miran sobre su gente
Como el sol de la mañana que
Sale de las sombras en la noche

1/22/97

Alegría

Alegría significa felicidad
Viene de la semilla de Amaranto
Bocado del tamaño de una goma borrador
Parece como un bloque solido llena de semillas
Solo tiene una pasita!
Con su nuez en el medio
Dándole sabor es como si fuera
El gusano en el Tequila

Vendida como una barra de caramelo
Por los ambulantes mercantiles de las calle
Alegría, es un bocado exquisito
Una merienda por las aceras populares de
La ciudad de Méjico.

1/22/99

Cuarto con Vista

Carmelitas y verdes
Sepia en los
Cementos
Los rascacielos
Modestos
Para la época moderna

Discos de marfil como
Antenas del televisor
Departamentos anaranjados
Automóviles de todos colores

Viéndolo todo desde la avenida
De los Bosques
La vista

La paleta del pintor
Dejando rasgo para la
Imaginación.

1/23/99

Hacienda de los Morales

Esta magnifica cantina
Se parece a un museo
De antigüedad con pasillos
Llenos de pinturas impresionistas
Con finos cuadros tallados
 De madera y metal

Hay mesas redondas para la
Cena de grandes familias y
Los patrones son serenados
Por los músicos Mariachi

Entre todas delicadezas
Están los gusanos fritos
Enrollados en sus fajitas
Con enchiladas o rellenados
Con salsa de hongo.

La riqueza del buen comer
En La casa de los Morales
Como sus nombres indican
Los patrones que son de
La clase rica.

El menú es diverso
Pasta, pescado, carne, servida
Con vegetales, ensalada y sopa.
Hay variedades de postres,
Pasteles y dulces finos.

Localizado cerca de la Ciudad de Méjico
Y sus exclusivas tiendas del distrito,
Es un contraste entre sus vistas vivas
Con sus musas de belleza y tristeza
De pobreza y riqueza
Cohabitando como un pez
En un gigantesco mar.
1/24/99

El Poder de la Metáfora

En el Palacio Nacional, un fresco, vivo
En la pared, como lagartija arrastrada
Avanza en el mundo Azteca de Diego Rivera
Fijando su medida en posición finito , mintiendo
Como el Merlín con su magia aromática
Mas anterior que un documento tangible.

Portentoso papel, el de la
Revolución Mejicana desde la
Invasión del Español hasta la
Liberación del trabajador
 Se queda en la muralla
Arrimada, el Marxista llamando
Desde el tríptico entre llamas
Como los colores del otoño.

Centinelas se paran erectos
Debajo su techo por la entrada
Del pórtico en los corredores del palacio

Los turistas inspirados se quedan
Mirando por largo tiempo la mano artística
 de Rivera o al sentido de contrabando una
Noción políticamente potente

Los guardias con sus uniformes verdes con
Rifles automático en hombros llevan en
Su casual paso preservando el orden y la ley

sin embargo, el mural se alimenta
Al incrédulo observar como una fiebre
Curiosa, mientras que la milicia mantiene
Su algo refuerzo entablado comiendo
De la ideología y del arte como una víbora
Y flautista debajo del mismo techo.

1/31/99

Miller Sobre La Mente Mejicana

Henry Miller, en las mentes
De los Mejicanos
Me han dicho
Era un héroe.
El Trópico de Cáncer,
Capricornio y más
Perforó sus impresiones
Como la música de Leonard
Cohen, salsa caliente, tortillas,
Sabor de pasión en la lengua
El gusano del tequila
Se desliza perenne por la garganta.

1/24/99

Plumas de Humo

Volcán activo en vista con
Su vapor ascendiendo
Como las ruinas ancianas
En el cielo matutino

La pista del Aeropuerto
Espera para que la pluma
De humos entre en ella

El suspiro del pasado
Como un sueño de horror
La venganza de la inquisición
Los Conquistadores

1/24/99

La Tierra Buena

La tierra buena
Tiene sus semillas
Otorgada por el árbol
Orgulloso,
Montañas descubiertas y
Respirando, están
Ascendiendo más de una milla
Hasta el cielo.

Encima de este lago mas de
20 millones patinan en autos,
En pies, o de cualquier modo
La tierra buena recoge y no condena
Encima de este lago 20 millones de
Vidas son transcendentes.

La tierra buena gruñe como
Una criatura con hambre y una
Boca que reconoce su necesidad para
Que le den de comer

La tierra buena no esconde mentiras
Por mucho tiempo.
Dos volcanes activos
La miran fijamente desde el valle

La tierra buena no esconde mentiras
Por mucho tiempo,
Como el ojo mirando la profundidad
Del barril de una pistola,
20 millones de mártires
Le cantan su canción.

La tierra buena retumba
Como truenos y relámpagos
Desde los terremotos debajo
De sus piscina de aguas

La tierra buena
Conoce sus obligaciones
Pero no distingue de aquellas
Personas que la cuidan

La tierra buena continua
Como una melodía cantada
Una canción reconocida
Por todos abajo en el valle.

1/24/99

Después Hablo El Papa

Dentro de un cartucho de Ruffles
Potato Chips esta estampa cuadrada
Estaba afuera para que la vieran
Todos los ojos.

Joven: No permitas que la violencia
Destruya la vida y la libertad
Del ser humano

Juan Pablo II

Este mensaje escrito en un papel
Cuadrado dentro de una bolsa
De meriendas de almuerzo
Fue entregado en el American Flight
Desde Ciudad de Méjico hasta Dallas
Y vino en el momento que el Papa
Iba a comenzar la misa del Domingo
En la Ciudad de Méjico el 24 de Enero
Del 1999

El 22 de Enero marcaba la cuarta visita
En el año que el Papa visitaba a el país
Cual le das mas apoyo al Vaticano que
Cualquier país en nuestro planeta

El rumor era que sería el fin de semana
Mas segura para caminar las calles
Dela ciudad

El día y la noche antes de la misa
Yo había visto prostitutas con sallas rojas
En las esquinas del distrito de la ciudad
Yo vi a los vendedores por las calles, y a niños
Vender chicles de Tridente
Una mujer malabarista entre el stress
Del trafico, niños lavando las ventanas de los automóviles
Vendiendo sus servicios
Gentes con sus campamientos en
La plaza central y nosotros

Al opuesto en el palacio Presidencial
Pero no vi ninguna acción de violencia
La semana que vino el Papa a la ciudad
Y anuqué yo no vi a el hombre santo
Sus palabras aparecían en un cartucho
De papitas fritas
Uno pudiera decir, sus palabras
Eran comida para el pensamiento…

1/24/99

Nativity / **Nelly Zamora Jones**

Beatriz Ezban

Una pintora de estatura pequeña
Una vez estudio a Monet,
Los clásicos, y también las inspiraciones
De William Blake,
Henry Miller,
Herman Melville, Las canciones de Leonard Cohen
Para nombrar unas cuantas

Su trabajo fue jurado
Por los alrededores de Méjico
Iceland, Westchester Pennsylvania,
Hong Kong y otros lugares

Ella es descendiente de Judíos Sirios
Una nativa de Méjico,
Su taller en casa,
En la Ciudad de Méjico.

Nos habíamos conocidos por medio
De nuestros primos,
Beatriz y Enrique
Nos encontramos paseando
Por las calles, sentados en los
Café al aire libre y encontramos
Lo común del toque personal
Los que nos une en nivel universal,
El dolor y lo divertido de la vida.

"El lenguaje es diferente pero
Las personas con sus necesidades y
Sus deseos son iguales"
Reveló ella.

Después tomando té de hierba
En las horas delicadas del día
Nosotros hablamos de Malcom Lowry
Y su libro, 'Under the Volcano' (Hundido en el Volcán)
Gabriel García Márquez, Octavio Paz,
Elizabeth Bishop, León Felipe,
Isabel Allende, Henry Miller,

Mas poetas, pintores, y tejedores de cuentos
Como la grabación de Leonard Cohen tocaba

"Todos Lo Saben" y la noche como
Cualquier otra noche se nos
Resbala calladitamente.

1/26/99

Ramat Shalom

Esta sinagoga ortodoxa
En la avenida Loma del Bosque
Esta situada el la montañosa
Parte del Oeste del valle

En este final del pueblo
Una enclave de residentes Judíos
Habitan

Hay un distrito del pueblo
Donde muchos vendedores judíos
Abrieron sus tiendas y se quedaron
A vivir antes, durante, y después de
La Segunda Guerra Mundial.

Hay 55,000 Judíos en Méjico, y
La mayoría de ellos 22,000
Viven en la Ciudad de Méjico.

Ramat Shalom es unos de los
Cuatro o seis templos en la
Ciudad reconstruido en el 1990
Es unos de los mas modernos
Prototípico Americano

Las mujeres están separadas de
Los hombres como instruye la
Tradición ortodoxa, es difícil
Que sus esposas acepten la oración
Que ellos recitan dando Gracias a Dios
Que ellos no nacieron mujer.

En Ramat Shalom como en muchas
Culturas latinas, aunque
No sea por religión- ortodoxia es la norma
En la comunidad judía predominante en
La ciudad de Méjico, ya que la tradición tiene
Sus raíces firmes. Los congregados tienen

Sus propias milicias, se pudiera decir. Ahí
Hombres voluntarios por sus sinagogas y sus
Esquinas cercanas en cada calle que se paran
En guardia los días del Sabbat. La vigilancia es imperativa.

1/27/99

El Nuevo Concepto En Cafés   (Tienda de Café)

Beatriz Ezban y Yo
Tomábamos   café y
Platicábamos en esta
Tienda de Café

Con sillas y bancos de
Metales retorcidos en los
Dispensarios de Café
Extendiéndose como vid,
En un diseño artistico

Era una clase de estación
Que un escritor pudiera
Hacer lo máximo con el poder
De la pluma y la observación

Toda ciudad tiene sus monumentos
Sus esquinas dilapidadas,
Grietas, rincones
Los barrios, bistrós,
Catedrales, parques,
Y distrito de vendedores (shopping)
El ojo del artista
Encuentra a su nido
Un lugar para descansar
Para invitar una fiesta
Ambulante

Un Nuevo Concepto En Cafés
Era como posarse en una rama
Para el Señor Hirsh

1/27/99

Fotografía Instantánea

El turista vio las torretas
Los techos de terracota,
Cúpulas, artefactos ornamentales,
En las iglesias, en las fachadas de
Los museos, edificios del gobierno

La piedra de lima avejentada
Fachadas por las plazas y
Corredores por las calles traseras
Que se veían algo triste

Pero nunca tan triste como
Ver a los niños, las mujeres,
Y hombres jovenes en las calles
Vendiendo chicles, caramelos, flores,
Maní, muñecas y globos, o una amoladora
De órganos cambiándose por dinero, o la mujer
Malabarista como un payaso entre trafico
Amenazante, o niños que lavan las ventanas
De los carros, la mujer decrepita
Extendiendo su mano como la
Mano de Miguel Ángelo en la capilla Sixtina,
Para obtener un indulto celestial

Los turistas no podían pensar en los Mejicanos
Campesinos como marionetas en un museo
O el 'clic' de un Polaroid con orgullo

Como palacios y arte
Ellos eran una parte que respiraban
La historias, el pasado y el presente,
Tejida en la tela de urbanidad,
Ciudad de Méjico, El tercero mundo,
Mas allá de estos bordes.

1/3/99

Todos Santos

En el museo
Habían mascaras y
Marionetas
Arboles de la vida y la muerte
Una banda de esqueletos
Tocando tambores y
Clarinetes

El festival de la muerte
Lo tratan como el gran afuera
No solo una conmemoración
Pero una gran reunión también

Almas de niños muertos
Vuelven en este día de
El día de los Muertos.

En el mes de Noviembre
Como costumbre Azteca
El noveno mes es dedicado a
Las almas infantiles y
El décimo mes a los adultos

El festival empezó el 31 de Octubre
El día de los angelitos,
O los pequeños ángeles

El boato se desamarra
Por la fiesta de San Andrés
O al final de Noviembre
Hasta llegar a Diciembre

Todos los Santos
Es Todos los Días de los Santos
Con sus trajes pintados de esqueletos
Y el borde del destripador guadaña
En exhibición
De esta manera la cultura honra
a sus almas vivientes y las que se han
Ido vestidos con sus trajes muy similar

2/13/99

Gol, Tocando abajo (Touchdown)

El avión salió del cielo
Hasta este aeropuerto
Modesto en medidas

Para la ciudad mas grande
Casi 22 millones de almas
El cuerpo de perpetuidad
En el valle de abajo

El volcán activo
La tierra de poca confianza
Nosotros tocamos abajo
Mientras que nos íbamos
Mas llenos y renacidos.

1/21/99

Man Leaning on Shadow | Lester Hirsh

Artists

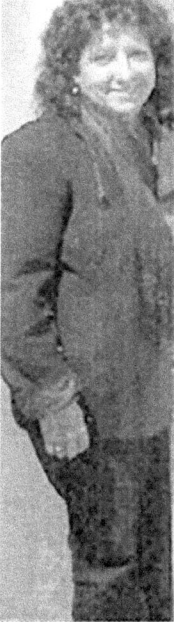

Nelly Zamora Jones
Artist/Translator

A native of Guines, Havana, Cuba, Nelly Zamora Jones and her family moved to the United States at the age of ten. Nelly is the recipient of the Cintas Fellowship Foundation Visual Arts,1976. She has traveled extensively in Europe and exhibited at the Salon of Contemporary Art in Paris, France,'85. Zamora Jones' work has been exhibited internationally. Visit Zamora Jones website for more info:

www.zamoraartproductions.com

Raquel Fruchter
Artist

Raquel Fruchter comes from an international family. Her father was born in Poland, her mother in Romania, her brother was born in Russia, and she in Havana, Cuba. The daughter of Jewish Holocaust survivors, Raquel emigrated to the US when she was nine years old, settling in Miami, Florida where she studied art. She has a degree in Fine Arts from the University of South Florida, a background in Arts Education, and has held the position of coordinator of Artists in the Schools Program at the Arts Council of Hillsborough County for the past 30 years.

Joseph McCann
Artist

Joseph McCann, studied art in New York at the Pratt Institute of Art, Queens College , and abroad in England and Europe. He holds a Bachelor of Fine Arts from the University of South Florida, and has exhibited his paintings in galleries in Florida and New York. His work reflects his interest in abstract imagery.

Joseph McCann | Raquel Fruchter | Lester Hirsh

Author

Lester Hirsh

musician, singer/songwriter, poet

Lester Hirsh is an established singer/songwriter and guitar player who has performed in a variety of venues from New Hampshire to Florida the past 40 years. He is also a published poet, former coeditor and publisher of *Bone & Flesh* magazine (1998-2002), a respected literary magazine of poetry, prose, essays and art from the finest writers nationally and internationally. He earned a Bachelor of General Studies/Literature, Granite State College, NH (1988)

Lester has performed solo and in a variety of ensembles over the years: the folk trio *Side Three* (Tampa, Florida) folk/pop duo *Jerusalem* (Williamsport PA) and duo *Sweet River* (Concord NH).

He has produced and recorded:

- three LP tapes—*Part & Parcel* (1986), *Piper's Dream* (1990), *Whistle in the Wind* (1994*)*;

- six CDs —*Tales of a Troubadour* (1994), *Sweet Surrender* (1998), *Strangers or Lonesome Friends* (2003), *Lester Hirsh Live* (2005), *Lester Hirsh at the Coffee & Tea Room* (2005) and *River of Strings* (2006);

- and the spoken word two CD set — *Mosaic II: Poems of an Ancient Order* (2005)

Hirsh also was a producer and the director of the *Summer Solstice Folk Festival* in Pottsville PA in 2007.

He was a finalist at the Napa Valley Emerging Songwriter Contest in 1997.

In 2005, Hirsh was a grammy nominee, for Best Spoken Word, for his volume of poems, *Mosaic II: Poems of an Ancient Order,* honored by the American Academy of Music. He was also featured on NPR New Hampshire Public Radio, Front Porch in 2002.

For details about the author's poetry, books and songs check the Preface of this book and his web page:

www.parisburg.com/lesterhirsh.html

His music can be purchased on www.cdbaby.com/all/troubadourpoet and through his web sites.

Links to Lester's live performance dates can be found at:

www.bignoisenow.com/hirsh.html